Meghan Rose
All Dressed up

written by
Lori Z. Scott

illustrated by
Stacy Curtis

Standard®
PUBLISHING
Bringing The Word to Life

Cincinnati, Ohio

Published by Standard Publishing, Cincinnati, Ohio
www.standardpub.com

Text Copyright © 2008 by Lori Z. Scott
Illustrations Copyright © 2008 by Stacy Curtis

Printed in: USA
Project editor: Laura Derico
Cover and interior design: Holli Conger

ISBN 978-0-7847-2106-3

Library of Congress Cataloging-in-Publication Data

Scott, Lori Z., 1965-
  Meghan Rose all dressed up / written by Lori Z. Scott;
illustrated by Stacy Curtis.
       p. cm.
  Summary: Meghan Rose feels bad because she does not have
designer clothes, and when she gets poison ivy she feels even
worse, but her grandmother reminds her that God loves her
for how she is on the inside, not how she looks on the outside.
Includes discussion questions and activities.
  ISBN 978-0-7847-2106-3 (perfect bound)
  [1. Beauty, Personal—Fiction. 2. Peer pressure—Fiction. 3.
Grandmothers—Fiction. 4. Christian life—Fiction.] I. Curtis,
Stacy, ill. II. Title.
  PZ7.S42675Mac 2008
  [Fic]—dc22
                                         2007049275

14 13 12 11 10 09 08   9 8 7 6 5 4 3 2 1

Contents

Fashion Show

Music blared. Speaking into a plastic microphone, my friend Lynette announced, "Ladies and stuffed animals! It's time for Meghan Rose's Fashion Show!"

My other friend Kayla clapped. I put my hands on my hips. She clapped more. I tapped my toe.

She clapped louder.

I pushed up my plastic crown and said, "Kayla! The lights!"

Kayla's mouth made a big letter O shape. She flicked the light switch up and down. The room flashed bright, dark, bright, dark, in beat with the music.

I spun around the room. My sparkly pink princess dress swirled around me like flower petals in the wind.

Finally Lynette shut off the music. She tightened a purple scarf around her neck. "My turn! You do the lights, Meghan."

Kayla grabbed the plastic microphone. "I'm the announcer."

Then the whole thing started over. Music blared. Kayla bellowed, "Ladies and stuffed animals! It's time for Lynette Becker's Fashion Show!"

And I flicked the lights.

Wowie! We sure have fun putting on fashion shows. Especially when we get all dressed up in Lynette's shimmery, glimmery play clothes. She owns dresses, fairy wings, crowns, necklaces, lacy gloves, plastic shoes, purses, wands, hats, umbrellas, and scarves.

Let me tell you—that kid is loaded.

I like Lynette. I used to not like her because when she sat in front of me at school I couldn't see over her big frilly hair bows.

Plus she made me nervous because she kept her school desk spotless. And I'm not certain that's normal.

But she makes a good friend. So I do not hold her frilly hair bows or clean desk against her.

I like Kayla too. Kayla is kangaroo bouncy and blue-eyed, like me. Plus, Kayla has blond hair that's usually piggy-tailed.

Except today Kayla wore a fancy,

floppy hat, so her piggy tails were smashed under it.

Just as Lynette's turn ended, her mom yelled from downstairs. "Girls! Time to clean up! I'm taking you home in fifteen minutes."

Lynette yelled back, "OK!"

That's when things went wrong. Because we had to take off all those beautiful clothes.

And put on our plain clothes.

Kayla squirmed into her bright orange jumper. I grabbed my jeans and white shirt off the pile of clothes on Lynette's bed. After pulling the shirt over my head, I yanked on my jeans.

I was tying my shoelaces when Lynette started getting dressed.

She paused. She smoothed down the shirt

she'd just put on. She touched the collar. Her eyebrows went up.

Then Lynette zoomed her brown eyes in on me and frowned. "You have on my shirt."

I looked from my shirt to hers. They looked the same.

I frowned back. "Not-huh."

Lynette nodded. "Yes, you do."

"Do not."

"Do too."

I stomped my foot. "How do you know? They look exactly alike."

Poking her finger at my chest, Lynette said, "Not *exactly*. Look right there."

My chest seemed to burn where Lynette pressed it.

Stepping back, I looked. I saw a tiny green pickle.

Lynette said, "My shirt has a pickle on it. I bought it at In the Pickle. But this shirt," she waved her hand over her front, "has no pickle. I'd never wear such a plain white shirt. I'm a Pickle-brand girl."

Kayla jumped up like an excited puppy. "Me too! I shopped at the Pickle store. And look! I have a pickle right here!" She pointed at her jumper. "I'm a Pickle-brand girl too!"

Lynette smiled.

I did not like that smile.

Not one bit.

"That means Kayla and I are fashion queens," Lynette said. "And you're not, Meghan Rose."

My face felt hot. "But my shirt looks just like yours!"

Lynette sniffed. "It's not a Pickle shirt."

Frustration whined out of me. "You can hardly even *see* the pickle!"

"So? Pickle is better than plain. Pickle clothes make you look special and pretty."

Kayla nodded. "Right. The Pickle is better. Even though Pickle clothes have the same ingredients as regular clothes. And you can hardly see the pickle."

Lynette held out her hand. "So give me back my shirt."

Feeling small, I pulled off the Pickle-brand shirt. I handed it over. I took my own ugly white shirt and slipped it on.

As we went downstairs, my whole body drooped down. Because how could I get all dressed up without Pickle clothes?

Pickles, Pickles Everywhere!

I never paid much attention to the Pickle store before. But that Monday in the classroom before school started, I saw Pickle stuff all over the place.

Abigail wore Pickle socks.

Ryan read a Pickle comic book.

Levi used a Pickle pencil.

Mallory had on a Pickle belt.

Kayla wore Pickle piggy-tail holders.

Adam hid a Pickle yo-yo in his desk.

Lynette showed off her Pickle bracelet.

Pickles, pickles, pickles! Pickle note-books. Pickle glue sticks (green glue—great idea!). Pickle lunch boxes. I bet someone was even wearing Pickle underwear!

In all, I counted seventeen Pickle things in the classroom. Where did they all come from?

More importantly, why didn't I own any Pickle things?

When morning announcements started, I squirmed in my seat. Did Adam think I looked gross without a Pickle shirt? Would Abigail avoid me because of my plain, un-Pickle socks?

Did everyone in the whole world know the truth about me? Did they know that I did not own Pickle clothes, Pickle gadgets, or Pickle ANYTHING?!

I did not feel special or pretty.

Instead, I wanted to hide under my seat.

During math, an idea popped *BLAM* into my head. After slipping a green marker into my pocket, I raised my hand. "Mrs. Arnold, can I go to the bathroom?"

Mrs. Arnold stopped in the middle of a sentence. "Can you wait until after math, Meghan? I'm introducing new material about acute angles."

Very polite, I said, "Yes, Mrs. Arnold. I can wait. But I don't want to."

Mrs. Arnold raised one eyebrow at me. I swallowed and slouched in my seat. "It's not that tangles aren't interesting. I just do not believe tangles are cute. I always pull them out with a hairbrush."

The corner of Mrs. Arnold's lip twitched

into a smile. She quick flattened her lip again. "I'm talking about an *acute angle*, not *a cute tangle*, Meghan Rose."

"Oh," I said. "What does it look like?"

Mrs. Arnold thought for a minute. "Picture an alligator with its mouth open."

She held her arms out straight, one over the other, palms almost touching. "From here," she stretched her arms far apart, "to here my arms form an acute angle."

My stomach tightened. "Do angles bite?"

Mrs. Arnold snapped her hands together, making me jump in my seat. She leaned toward my desk with a toothy smile. "No," she said. "But I might."

So I waited until the end of math to go to the bathroom because Mrs. Arnold is full of surprises.

Plus, she has a fine set of chompers in her mouth.

And I'm not taking any chances.

Once I was in the bathroom, I popped the cap off the green marker and drew a pickle on my shirt.

Except it looked more like a fat, fat sausage.

I crossed it out. I tried again.

Better. This time it looked like just a fat sausage.

I rubbed it with my fingers.

Now my yellow shirt had a fat, fat, fat green marker smudge on it.

Plus my fingers were green.

I twisted my shirt around and, for a moment, thrashed around in a cute tangle. Finally, I tugged my shirt on backwards.

Picking up the marker again, I made

another pickle. Small. Green.

"Perfect," I said, tucking the marker back in my pocket. Straightening my shoulders, I took a big breath. I walked back to the classroom with my head held high.

I felt special! I felt pretty! Because now I was a Pickle-brand girl too.

In a Pickle

At lunch recess, I showed Kayla my shirt.

Kayla squealed. "I can't believe you've got a Pickle shirt too!" She gave me a way-to-go kind of push in the back.

I'd know that push anywhere. I grinned. "I know. I'm all dressed up now."

Bouncing on her toes with excitement, Kayla said, "Me too!"

"I made up a new jump rope chant to celebrate," I said. "Listen."

I started jumping.

"I found five pennies
by a sycamore tree.
Five shiny pennies
for me, me, me!
I traded those pennies
for one gray nickel,
Went to the store to buy
one fat pickle.
So many pickles there,
my, oh, my!
How many pickles did I buy?
One, two, three . . ."

Kayla caught on fast. We chanted and laughed and jumped and chanted and laughed and jumped.

About the millionth time through, Lynette

joined us. But she didn't jump. She listened with her head cocked. Her jump rope hung at her side like a whip.

She held up a stop hand. "What's going on?"

My heart sped up. *BUMP-bump*. My face got hot. I tripped on my rope. The handle ripped out of my hand and smacked around my legs. *WHACK-whack*.

Once again, I was a cute tangle.

Kayla said, "Meghan made up a pickle chant since she's a Pickle girl now too."

Lynette gave me a sour-pickle look.

"Yep." I pointed at my shirt. "Here's my Pickle. That's why we needed a pickle chant."

Frowning, Lynette said, "Oh, really? And how does that go again?"

Kayla and I looked at each other and

shrugged. We got the beat going. *Thump, thump, thump, thump*.

"I found five pennies
by a sycamore tree.
Five shiny pennies
for me, me, me!
I traded those pennies
for one gray nickel,
Went to the store to buy—"

"A GREEN MARKER TO DRAW A
FAKE PICKLE ON MY SHIRT!" Lynette
shouted.

I stopped jumping and glared at her.

Lynette glared back.

Kayla kept on jumping.

Finally I looked away. "That's not how it
goes," I said in a voice just for Lynette.

"Faker," Lynette shot back.

My body went all droopy again.

I no longer felt special or pretty. "I don't want to jump rope anymore," I said.

"Good," Lynette said, folding her arms. "Because I don't want to play with a fake Pickle-brand girl."

Kayla jumped past. She was counting, "Twenty-eight, twenty-nine, twenty-ten . . ."

"Thirty," Lynette automatically corrected her. "Twenty-nine, thirty."

Then she narrowed her eyes at me.

"Kayla got it wrong. And so did you."

Dropping my rope, I ran off.

I ran all the way over to the far side of the playground.

I found Ryan kneeling in the grass. "Can I play with you?" I panted.

He looked up. "Why?"

"Just because."

Ryan shrugged. "Sure. But I'm not playing. I'm hunting for four-leaf clovers."

"Why?"

"Just because."

That's one thing I like about Ryan. He makes a lot of sense.

I bent over the patch of grass. Part of me looked through the clovers. Three-leaf. Three-leaf. Three-leaf.

The other part of me started to feel like a balloon about to explode.

I bit my lip. "Do you care if I'm not wearing Pickle clothes?" I blurted.

"No," Ryan said.

Just like you let the air out of a balloon with a *pssshhhhh*, my body relaxed.

Then, I saw it! A four-leaf clover.

I yanked it out. "I found one! I found one! I found a four-leaf clover."

Ryan took it from me and turned it over in his hands. "Sorry. This is a fake." He pointed at it. "This leaf split in two. See? So it looks like a four-leaf clover, but it's really just a plain old three-leaf clover."

He tossed the fake four-leaf clover aside. "Fakes are no good."

I swallowed. Hard. And slouched my shoulders.

I said, "I think I'll look over by the fence." It seemed like a better spot.

Away from everyone.

Ryan nodded. "OK. But I don't think there's so much clover over there. They are weird-looking clovers, if that's what they are. They're a lot bigger. Plus, the leaves are pointy and shiny and some are turning kind of rusty-colored. Weird."

"I'll fit right in then," I mumbled.

I plopped down on the ground. Part of me looked through the giant clovers. Three-leaf. Three-leaf. Three-leaf.

The other part of me started to itch.

Itchy, Splotchy, Whatcha Gotchy?

On the bus ride home after school, my itchiness increased.

I scratched at my arms like a dog with fleas. My fingernails left pink stripes on my skin. I wondered about poor, itchy dogs. How do they reach their tail ends? What if their bellies itch? Dogs must go nuts without fingers.

Being an itchy fishy would be worse

though, I believe. At least dogs have paws. How do fish scratch?

Snails! That's another animal that would have serious trouble scratching.

Poor guys.

Ryan interrupted my thoughts. "What's wrong with you?"

Turning sideways, I showed him my arm. "I'm itchy and splotchy."

Ryan leaned away from me. "Yuck! Whatcha got?"

I scratched again. "I don't know. Maybe mosquito bites?"

"I don't think so," Ryan said. "Unless a pack of those bloodsuckers held a party on your arm. Maybe you're mutating into a comic-book chicken. Then you can join the Poultry Gang and use your fowl feathers as a tickle weapon against Super Cat."

"Argh!" I said, scratching harder.

"That's it! I'm moving," Ryan said, scooting over to the seat across the aisle.

I turned my back to him and glared out the window. "Fine," I said, very grumpy. And itchy. I scratched my neck. Glad I'm not a dog. Or a fish. Or a snail.

Ryan said, "By the way, it's on your neck too."

"Argh!" I said again.

By bedtime the splotchy patches on my arms had grown bigger.

And they itched! Itchy, itchy, itchy! *ARRRRRRRGGGGHHHH!*

Mom noticed my scratching. She pulled up my pajama sleeve. "Where did you get this?" she asked.

"Get what?"

"Poison ivy."

I rubbed my arms. "I don't know. Did you say *poison*?"

Mom said, "Don't touch it! It'll spread. Let me look at you."

Mom inspected my arms. I sat very still and tried not to scratch.

Guess what? Telling an itchy person not to scratch is like setting a ball on a hill and telling it not to roll. Or putting chocolate in a hot car and telling it not to melt. Or giving my teacher, Mrs. Arnold, a red pen and telling her not to grade with it.

You just can't stop it from happening.

Mom made a *tsk-tsk* sound. "Not too bad. Yet. I'll put some cream on it. Most of it's on your arms, although your hands seem clear. I spy a few spots on your forehead, maybe where you pushed your hair away after touching the poison ivy."

I sniffled. "Will I be OK?"

Mom patted my leg. "You'll live. But if it gets worse, you'll have to see the doctor, just to be safe. For now, I think I'll keep you home from school tomorrow. Grandma Wright can watch you since I have to work."

That idea cheered me up. Grandma and I always have a blast together.

"What about Grandpa? Can he come?"

Mom shook her head. "He's fishing in Michigan this week."

"Oh," I said in a small voice.

Mom kept looking me over. "You must have gotten into a patch of poison ivy on the playground, I guess."

The playground? I bit my lip. "What does poison ivy look like?"

"It's a green plant with three pointy leaves. Sometimes the leaves look waxy and in the autumn they turn reddish."

Uh-oh, I thought.

"It can grow on the ground or climb around trees or fences—places like that. Did you find any of that?" Mom asked.

"Yes."

Frowning, Mom continued. "I sure hope this doesn't spread over your face. After all, school picture day is Thursday."

My heart went *bump-bump, bump-bump.*

Mom didn't notice. "I'll go get that cream. Don't scratch while I'm gone."

After she left, I flopped onto my bed. *School picture day?!* And now not only did I not own the right clothes, I had itchy, splotchy skin!

Ugly has a new name. Poison Ivy. And its last name is Pickle-less.

Poison Ivy Pickle-less. That's me.

Snickerdoodles and Riding Hoods

The next morning, I chewed my cereal extra loud. It made *crunch, crunch, crunch* sounds, like a car driving over gravel. Then *ding-dong,* the doorbell rang!

Dropping my spoon with a clang, I rocketed to the front door and ripped it open.

There stood Grandma. When she saw me, her whole face broke into a smile.

"Hello, princess!" she said. She threw her arms wide, and I threw myself into them for a hug.

I love everything about Grandma.

I love her blue eyes. If eyes could talk, hers would shout. They zap you with their power, like flashlight beams piercing a black night.

Also, the sprinkles of wrinkles covering her face seem to be linked to her eyes. Because when her eyes twinkle and blinkle with excitement, her wrinkles crinkle up into a smile.

I also love Grandma's reddish-brownish hair. It curls a little, and it's splattered with white. On rainy days, her hair gets frizzy. Sometimes she wears a scarf on her head to keep the frizzes under control.

Sometimes Grandma tells me I need to

wear a scarf on my body to keep it under control. But she laughs when she says it.

Most of all, I love Grandma's hands. She works hard gardening, cleaning, knitting, and keeping busy. So they are all knobby and rough, like the bark of an old oak tree.

But when she touches you, they feel warm and gentle.

Grandma is another lady who's full of surprises.

Clicking her car keys together, Mom came up behind us. She wore black pants, flat-heeled shoes, a striped blouse, and a silver necklace. She smelled like vanilla.

"You got all dressed up," Grandma said.

Mom smiled. "Thanks for coming. Call my cell phone if you need me."

Then Mom gave me a quick, lipsticky

kiss. "Bye! Listen to Grandma. I'll be home by three. And don't scratch."

I nodded, rubbing the red kiss print off my cheek. "OK. Bye, Mom."

Grabbing Grandma by the hand, I led her to the kitchen. "I'm done with breakfast," I said. "Let's make snickerdoodle cookies."

Grandma pursed her lips. She does that sometimes when she's thinking. Or when she's pretending to think but is actually being sneaky. "Sounds fun, but there's a problem. I'm fresh out of snickers. Maybe you could tell me a joke."

"Grandma!" I said in a don't-be-so-silly tone of voice.

Grandma shook her head. "I can't make snickers without a joke."

"OK," I said. I thought for a minute. "Why did the cookie go to the doctor?"

Grandma shrugged. "I don't know."

"Because it felt crumb-y!" I said. "Get it? Cookies have crumbs."

"Funny! Here are your snickers," Grandma said, and she laughed *ha-ha*. I pretended to catch each *ha* in my hands.

Holding my snickers close, I pursed my lips. I do that sometimes when I'm thinking. Or when I'm pretending to think but am actually being sneaky. "There is still a problem. Snickers aren't enough. We need some doodles."

"Oh, no!" Grandma said. "You're right! What will we do?"

I grinned as big as Texas. "I have paper and markers."

Grandma clapped. "Then what are we waiting for? Let's doodle."

And that's how our day started. After

snickering and doodling, Grandma and I baked real snickerdoodle cookies. They came out of the oven, all warm and cinnamony, and we each ate two.

Except I ate five.

Or six, possibly.

Next, Grandma and I thumb wrestled. Grandma mostly won since her thumbs are gigantic compared to mine. I am not certain that's fair.

Later, I snuggled on the couch with Grandma. She read *Little Red Riding Hood* to me.

That story reminded me about my problem.

So when Grandma finished the story, I sniffled.

Grandma squeezed my shoulder. "What's wrong?"

"That book made me sad."

Grandma looked puzzled. "But why? The woodcutter saves Little Red Riding Hood and her grandmother."

"Well," I explained, "The real problem wasn't the wolf at all. It was that Little Red didn't have any Pickle-brand clothes to wear. So she couldn't really get all dressed up to see Grandma. Instead she had to wear that plain hooded shirt."

"What?" Grandma said.

"Plus, I bet she cut through the woods so no one would see her ugly clothes. And when she did that, I'm sure she got poison ivy."

"Poison ivy? Pickles?" Grandma said.

"Exactly," I said. "In fact, I believe that's how she really got her name. She's a little red from scratching too much. And she's wearing a plain old Pickle-less hooded shirt. Little Red Hood. Or Poison Ivy Pickle-less. Same thing."

I thought for a minute. "But I believe that riding part of her name is a mix-up. Because Little Red Hood didn't actually ride anything. And who has two middle names anyway?"

Shaking her head, Grandma set the book down. "I'm completely lost."

I patted her leg. "Don't worry, Grandma. I know where you are."

Doctor Hoskins

Wednesday morning, the poison ivy on my forehead looked worse. Mom decided to take me to the doctor to get a shot.

I like Doctor Hoskins. He reminds me of Grandpa Wright except Doctor Hoskins has more gray hair. But they both wear glasses, have nice smiles, wrinkles, clever-looking eyes, and chuckle laughs.

I don't like his nurse.

Doctor Hoskins may say, "Meghan Rose,

my dear brave girl, it's time for a shot."

But then he leaves.

And his nurse comes back with a FAKE smile and a REAL needle.

I hate shots.

· I'd rather eat mud.

Mom dragged me to the car. As she buckled up, she said, "I'm sorry you have to miss another day of school."

I nodded, feeling cookie crummy.

Mom glanced in the rearview mirror. "I know you don't like shots. But I'm worried the poison ivy might spread. You don't want your eyes to swell shut, do you?"

Crossing my arms, I said, "No." But I didn't complain. After all, my mom had a point.

Only problem was, so would the nurse. A very sharpish, needle kind of point.

When we got there, some people were already waiting in the reception area. One couple sat by a basket. The man leaned over and made a cooing sound. A little hand reached out from the basket and grabbed his finger. I heard a happy gurgle, and the father smiled.

A little boy, maybe three years old, played with blocks at a small table. His nose looked snotty, and he kept wiping it on his sleeve. He banged the blocks together. *WHAM! WHAM! WHAM!*

His mother sat nearby flipping through a magazine. I guess the noise didn't bother her.

But it bothered me.

After all, the kid had no beat.

So while Mom signed in, I sat down at the table by him. "Excuse me, but you're doing it wrong," I said, very polite.

The boy stopped. He stared at me with big round eyes. He glanced back at his mother. She ignored him.

I held out my hand. "Can I try?"

The boy clutched the blocks to his chest and took a step backward.

I said. "Please?"

Squeezing the blocks tighter, he shook his head.

I sighed. "Fine. What's your name?"

"Wobert."

"Robert, you're a skilled whammer, but you lack style. Try whamming like this."

On the tabletop I drummed my fingers *tap-tap-tappity-tap-tap*.

Cocking his head, Robert smiled.

I did it again. *Tap-tap-tappity-tap-tap*. "You try," I said.

WHAM! WHAM! went Robert.

He didn't get it. I showed him again. *Tap-tap-tappity-tap-tap!*

WHAM! WHAM! went Robert as soon as I finished.

"Hey!" I said. "That's kind of catchy! Can you *WHAM WHAM* again?"

Giggling, Robert nodded.

I tapped, then Robert whammed.

Tap-tap-tappity-tap-tap. WHAM! WHAM!

Tap-tap-tappity-tap-tap. WHAM! WHAM!

Robert squealed with laughter.

Tap-tap-tappity-tap-tap. WHAM! WHAM!

Tap-tap-tappity-tap-tap. WHAM! WHAM!

We swayed to the beat!

Tap-tap-tappity-tap-tap. WHAM! WHAM!

Tap-tap-tappity-tap-tap. WHAM! WHAM!

Faster and faster and louder and louder we pounded out a rocking beat. We stopped when a nurse called, "Robert Browning."

Tossing down her magazine, Robert's mother stood. "That's us. Put the blocks down, Robert. Now."

Robert snatched them close again.

His mother frowned.

I said, "I'll watch them for you, Robert."

Like a bottle dripping out glue, Robert slowly handed me the blocks. Without a pause his mom strode off, pulling Robert along by his hand.

After that, I sat by Mom and waited.

And waited.

I hate waiting.

I slouched. And chewed on my fingernails. Since Robert left, I didn't have anything else to distract me. Besides my fingernails, that is.

In fact, I chewed one nail just for Robert. Plus I prayed in my head for both of us: *Dear God, please help my poison ivy get better. And please help Robert feel better too.*

Scratching my neck, I picked up the magazine Robert's mom left behind. It was crammed with pictures of beautiful people with beautiful smiles holding beautiful things and wearing beautiful clothes. The most beautiful ads of all were the Pickle-brand ones.

The more pages I turned in the magazine, the more I disliked my *blah* clothes and my *blah* hair and my *blah* itchy poison ivy skin.

A nurse called, "Erika Kerrman."

The couple with the baby lifted the basket and stood.

The nurse gasped. "How sweet! She's

sleeping. I love her little dress! How precious."

It must have been a Pickle dress.

When the nurse finally called my name, she didn't say the words *sweet* or *precious*. She said, "I bet that itches."

Glaring at her, I nodded. I didn't trust my mouth not to growl, so I kept it shut.

Mom and I trudged after her, down a long, narrow hallway to a small room.

After taking my temperature, the nurse said, "Get undressed and put on one of these gowns. The doctor will be here soon."

By the way, ever notice how nurses always promise that the doctor will be there soon and he never is? Nurses need better watches, I believe. I had enough time to trace all the blue wallpaper flowers with my pinky finger, jump off a chair twelve times, inflate a latex glove, and read the eye chart while standing on my head—all before the doctor came.

Finally, the door opened. "Doctor Hoskins!" I screamed.

I launched myself at him.

He was nice enough to catch me. "How's my favorite patient?"

The smile fell off my face. "Itchy."

He nodded. "Poison ivy, I hear."

Swallowing, I looked down. "Ugly."

Doctor Hoskins lifted my chin with his finger. "Wrong. Beautiful."

"Poison ivy is ugly," I insisted. I tugged at my gown. "So is this."

Doctor Hoskins winked. "Sure they are. But all dressed up in that poison ivy and ugly gown, I see a healthy, happy, bright-eyed girl. So I say beautiful."

I love that guy.

My whole body felt like one big smile after that. One big itchy smile.

You know, Doctor Hoskins is a sharp man.

Needles are sharp too.

And his nurse used one on my backside.

Picture Day

Mom smoothed down my hair. She gave a loud sigh. "Picture day—and this one piece of hair keeps sticking up like a cat's tail!"

Pushing her hand away, I said, "It doesn't matter. I'm getting retakes because of the poison ivy on my face."

Mom frowned. She sprayed my hair and smoothed it down again. "Except they never use retake pictures in the yearbook. That's why we got you all dressed up anyway."

49

My stomach did an elevator flop. "Really?" I croaked.

Mom didn't seem to hear me. "I spy the bus at Ryan's house. We'd better hustle out there or you'll miss it."

Right then, missing the bus sounded like a good idea to me.

But not to Mom.

She carried my backpack all the way to the curb before helping me slip it on. "Have a picture-perfect day!" she joked as the bus pulled up.

Right. A picture-perfect day. With poison ivy and Pickle-less clothes.

Somehow, I just couldn't picture it.

The school looked shiny and clean when we arrived. The janitors had probably dressed it all up too, just like everyone got all dressed up for picture day. As I hung up my backpack, I heard kids chattering in fast, excited voices.

Some of the kids moved like stiff robots, afraid to mess up their clothes.

Not Kayla, of course. I spotted her across the room bouncing around Mrs. Arnold like a puppy after its chew toy.

I studied smiling faces, curly hair, ribbons, button-down shirts, ties, black leather shoes (the kind that leave scuff marks on the gym floor), and lacy dresses. I noticed that some girls (like Lynette) even had a little makeup on.

I touched the bumps on my face, then jerked my hand away.

Something had to be done.

Before morning announcements started, I snuck to the sink. I lathered up my hands until they burst with bubbles. I scrubbed and scrubbed and scrubbed my face.

The poison ivy did not scrub off.

Mrs. Arnold came over. She did not look happy. "Meghan, what are you doing? Dry off your face and sit down, please."

I rubbed and rubbed and rubbed my face with a paper towel.

The poison ivy did not rub off.

I still had one thing left to try. With a green marker from my desk, I quickly drew a tiny pickle on my hand. Maybe the pickle would make me feel pretty.

It didn't.

After announcements, Mrs. Arnold said, "Class, you're getting your pictures taken today." She strolled around our desks. "No doubt your parents will hang your picture on the wall. If you compare it to last year's kindergarten picture, you might be surprised at how much older you look."

Kayla interrupted, "Or how much cuter we look!"

Lynette said, "Or how much more stylish we look."

Kids started whispering to each other. I slouched wa-aaaay down in my seat.

Mrs. Arnold raised a finger. Everyone quieted.

"A year from now, when you're in second grade, the school will take your picture again," she said. "No doubt your parents will hang that picture up too. And you'll probably look back at this first-grade picture and be surprised at how much you changed in one year."

Mrs. Arnold continued. "Now, what do you think your picture will look like when you are seventy-five years old?"

Kayla raised her hand. "Will we be in high school by then?"

Mrs. Arnold laughed. "You'll be a grandma by then, dear."

Kayla gasped.

Passing out papers, Mrs. Arnold said, "Your writing assignment today is to draw a picture of what you will look like when you're seventy-five years old. Write three to five sentences about your drawing. You have twenty minutes to work before we line up for pictures."

Mrs. Arnold is a master at getting you all interested and thinking and excited about ideas and then *whammo*—giving you an assignment.

She's a tricky one.

But so am I.

I stuffed that assignment way in the back of my desk.

Maybe when Mrs. Arnold is seventy-five, she'll find it.

The Big, Bad, Picture Lady

Twenty minutes later, we walked down to the gym for pictures. We lined up by height, from shortest to tallest, so Mrs. Arnold put me near the end of the line. Kayla and Lynette stood way up front.

While we waited, Mrs. Arnold checked everyone's collars, ties, and hair. Soon, a super sugary, high-pitched voice said, "Are you ready, Mrs. Arnold? You look so lovely."

Tittering, Mrs. Arnold disappeared behind a screen.

A big flash lit the room, and that syrupy voice said, "Next."

I strained my ears. The voice shrilled, "Hello, princess. Smile."

Flash! "Next!"

The voice continued to squawk out compliments. "Hello, handsome. Sit tall."

Flash! "Next!"

The voice used friendly words. But it almost sounded impatient. Bored. "Hello, cupcake. Hold it."

Flash! "Next!"

In fact, the picture lady's voice sounded a little scary.

I bet that picture lady has squinty eyes and maybe a wart on the end of her long pointy nose. She probably has crooked yellow teeth. And I'm sure her hair has bird nests in it.

Poor Kayla went next.

The voice spoke. "Hello, superstar. Sit tall. Smile. Stop moving." The voice got grumpy. "Leave the pigtails alone. Smile. Too big. No making faces. Better. Smile."

Flash! "Next!"

The line shrank with each flash. Step-by-step my turn approached. After the last student before me went, that nasty voice called, "Next!"

I scrambled over to the seat, plopped down, and yanked

my turtleneck up over my face.

The voice ordered, "Pull your sweater down."

But I was afraid. Afraid to get my picture taken and afraid to see the person who owned the evil-sounding voice. So I shook my head.

The voice coaxed. "Show me your pretty smile."

Just like a snake, that voice. I shook my head harder.

The voice sounded mad. "Pull that sweater down now!"

"No!" I yelled.

Next thing I knew, something yanked my sweater. My head popped out. And I saw a pair of angry, green eyes blazing at me.

The picture lady!

But she wasn't ugly at all. She wore a long, navy skirt dotted with small, purple flowers. A silky, matching purple blouse. Navy high-heeled shoes. Three gold rings. A gold necklace with a heart charm. Her red hair looked freshly curled. She had on lipstick and eye shadow. Her hands had long nails with square tips, all painted with rich purple nail polish.

She was so, so, so beautiful.

I gaped at her. How could she sound so ugly and look so beautiful? How could her smile look so warm, but her eyes look so cold?

Was she like the wolf in *Little Red Riding Hood*? All dressed up like someone special, but still a wolf underneath that granny nightgown?

Tears filled up my eyes and spilled out onto my cheeks.

The camera flashed, and I ran out of the room.

The rest of my day didn't go any better.

Mrs. Arnold found my crumpled assignment. She kept me inside for lunch and recess, so I didn't see my friends.

Plus, she sent the work home with a note.

The YOU You

When the bus picked me up Friday morning, I worried. I had survived the picture lady, but I still had red patches of poison ivy. I still didn't have Pickle-brand clothes.

What would everyone think about how I looked?

Worse, I hadn't talked to Lynette and Kayla since Lynette and I fought during Monday's recess.

With my head down, I stumbled to my

seat. At least no one screamed when I went by. Or pointed. Or laughed. Or fainted in horror.

Or threw up.

Sighing with relief, I dropped down next to Ryan. He was reading a Super Cat comic book. Good old Ryan.

Then I noticed his T-shirt. It had a big green pickle on it.

Shrinking back, I covered up my own shirt with my backpack.

I cleared my throat. "Hi."

Ryan lowered his comic book. "It's you!"

"It's me."

"What's up?"

"Nothing. You?"

Ryan held out his book. "Super Cat."

I shrugged. "Super Cat?"

"New," Ryan said.

I sat up, "Brand new?"

Ryan grinned. "Brand new."

That's one thing I like about Ryan. He's easy to talk to. We read the new Super Cat story together all the way to school.

I didn't say much at school all morning. I believe that made Mrs. Arnold nervous. For no reason, she'd pick up her red pen and twirl it through her fingers. Plus she'd glance at me and pause, wait, then raise one eyebrow and go on with the lesson.

Meanwhile, I tried not to scratch.

Instead I counted Pickle things in the classroom. Twenty. Lynette had three.

I counted poison ivy patches on arms. Five. I had all of them.

I counted the minutes until lunch. Thirty.

Minutes until lunch recess. Forty-five.

Minutes until I found out whether or not Lynette and Kayla would play with me. Not enough.

That's why I sat by myself at lunch. When lunch recess rolled around, I headed straight for the swing set. If you can pump your legs, you don't need a friend.

As I swung forward, backward, forward, backward, I prayed. I don't even remember what I prayed, I just prayed. I didn't have anyone else to talk to, and God always listens. He listens even when you don't actually remember what to say.

I believe maybe God listens so well because he isn't easily distracted. He doesn't look at your skin. Even if you've got itchy poison ivy skin.

And he doesn't look at your clothes. Or

call you a fake Pickle-brand girl.

No, I think God listens because he sees and loves the YOU you.

The sad, boo-hoo you. The happy, we're-going-to-the-zoo-zoo-zoo you. The confused I-just-don't-know-what-to-do you.

Like Doctor Hoskins, God lifts you up and says, "Beautiful." Even if you feel Poison Ivy Pickle-less ugly.

Too bad not everybody sees like that.

My swing slowed to a stop as I dragged one foot on the ground. I scanned the playground for my friends.

Two hands pushed on my back, setting me in motion again.

My heart soared. I'd know that push anywhere.

"Kayla!" I squealed.

"Meghan!" Kayla squealed back. She

gave me another push. "I missed you. Why didn't you eat lunch with us? Or come play jump rope?"

"Just because," I said.

I closed my eyes and smiled and let the air zip by. Forward. Backward.

Another voice said, "Push me too, Kayla."

Could it be? I peeked. Lynette sat on the swing next to me.

"Hi," I said, zooming forward.

Lynette squinted at me. "Still don't have Pickle clothes?"

"No," I said, zooming back.

"Still have poison ivy?"

"A little," I said. "Still want to swing with me?"

My stomach did a flip when Lynette didn't answer right away. Then Kayla gave

Lynette a hard push. She started swinging.

We swung opposite. First I swung high and her low, then the other way round.

Pumping harder, Lynette finally said, "Sure, I'll swing with you."

I swallowed. "Why?"

Lynette *whooshed* back. "Just because."

"Yeah," Kayla echoed. "Just because!"

That's one thing I like about Lynette and Kayla. They make a lot of sense.

Kicking my feet off the ground, I rocketed high to match Lynette's swing. Together we swung, forward and backward, side by side, giggle by giggle.

I prayed in my head. *Thanks, God. I'm glad you gave us good friends that see and love the YOU you too.*

Under the Hood

Friday night, Mom and Dad had a date.

That means they got all dressed up and went to a fancy restaurant.

Fancy restaurant means they use towels instead of paper napkins. Also there are no ketchup bottles on the table. Plus you can't supersize your order.

They go once a month and Grandma Wright stays with me.

After Mom gave me one last lipsticky

kiss and Dad swept me into a hug and they both went out the door, I turned to Grandma.

I had one thing on my mind. "Grandma, let's play beauty shop."

Grandma's mouth made a long thin line. "Oh, joy," she said in a voice like a flat tire.

Placing my play makeup box down on the kitchen table next to Grandma, I said, "Who would you like to look like today, Grandma?"

Grandma chuckled. "Myself. But if I have to look like someone else —"

I interrupted because I had already planned it all out. "I'll make you into a Pickle model."

Grandma frowned. "I don't know. What does a Pickle model look like?"

"They have long green hair, big green eyes, green lipstick, green earrings, green nail polish, and a thin body."

Grandma whistled. "That will take a lot of fixing up."

"You got that right," I said. With quick strokes, I brushed her hair. "Compared to the Pickle models, you're kind of like a busted, rusted, old red pickup truck. But I do not hold that against you."

Sitting up straight, Grandma said, "Just remember this little red pickup truck has a pretty good motor under the hood."

I paused. "What do you mean?"

"Well, the outside may not look like much. But on the inside, I'm a beauty. I feel shiny new."

Now, I thought about that for a minute. And I decided Grandma probably meant she had swallowed some soap and rinsed it down with water to get her insides shiny clean. After all, if you wash a car with soap, it really shines.

Then an idea popped *BLAM* into my head. "So if you're a little red truck with a hood and you drive someplace . . ."

Grandma nodded. "That's right. I'm a little red riding hood."

We both laughed.

Grandma is a hoot.

I snapped green barrettes into her hair. I rubbed red circles on her cheeks. I put green eye shadow on her. I painted her fingernails lime green. I rubbed shiny body glitter on her forehead and nose. I draped a green scarf around her shoulders.

When I finished, I said, "Ta-da! You're all dressed up now."

Grandma said, "How do I look?"

I studied her face. Grandma wriggled her eyebrows at me and made me laugh. "Stop it, Grandma. I'm checking you out."

Finally I sighed. "I did my best. But you don't look anything like a Pickle model. For one thing, you've got all those wrinkles."

Grandma touched her face. "True. But I wouldn't trade these wrinkles for anything. They remind me of the smiles God has brought into my life. And all the worries he's carried me through."

I shrugged. "Fine. But your nose is much too big."

"Oh, really?" Grandma said. She pulled me close. She made her voice low. "The better to smell you with, my dear."

She snuffled at my neck. I squealed and giggled.

Lifting me into her lap, Grandma asked, "Is there anything else you don't like about the way I look?"

"Your chin," I pointed. "You've got an extra circle on it."

Grandma growled again. "It's called a dimple. And it's the better to tickle you with, my dear!"

Jiggling her jaw, she tickled my back with her chin. I squealed and giggled. "Anything else?" she said.

"Did you know your ears hang low?"

"And they wobble to and fro," Grandma said. "I can tie 'em in a knot. I can tie 'em in a bow."

I waited. "Well?"

Grandma smiled. "The better to hear you with, my dear." Her face got serious. "You need to hear me too, Meghan Rose.

75

You may not like my wrinkles, or my nose, or my chin, or my ears. But this is the face God gave me. And I don't think I'll change a thing."

I stared at my grandma with her twinkly-wrinkly-crinkly face. And I understood something, like when someone tells a joke and all of a sudden you get it.

When you really, finally understand, just figuring it out makes you so happy, your toes start tingling, and the tingle goes all the way to your belly where a big laugh bubbles up and explodes from your mouth with a loud *HA*.

That kind of *get it*.

I threw my arms around Grandma's neck. "Oh, Grandma, of course you shouldn't change your face. You're the most beautiful grandma in the whole world."

Grandma hugged me close. "I don't know what you're looking at, sweetie," she said with a muffled voice. "But it sure isn't my face."

"No, Grandma. I'm looking under the hood. You're sweet and kind and funny and snuggly and smiley and nice. Plus you smell like powder."

I pressed her rough, tree-bark hands against my cheek.

I love those hands.

They are so, so beautiful.

All Dressed Up

Saturday morning, I pulled out my assignment. Mom said I had to finish it before I could call my friends over to play.

Plopping down in a seat at the kitchen table, I smoothed down the crumpled edges of the paper. I stared at the directions. *Draw a picture of what you will look like when you are seventy-five years old. Then write three to five sentences about your picture.*

With a sigh, I slouched in my seat.

Mrs. Arnold sure gives tough assignments.

And, *argh*! Would this itchy poison ivy ever go away?

Scratching thoughtfully with one hand, I picked up my pencil with the other.

I stopped.

My hands.

My fingernails did not have squared tips and purple nail polish like the picture lady. In fact, I had chewed off most of my nails during my doctor's visit when I prayed for Robert.

I did not have shiny gold rings on my fingers. In fact, I had a skinned knuckle from playing basketball with Ryan last week.

My palms were not clean and smooth. In fact, they had dirt on them from helping my mom clean up the floor after breakfast.

I smiled. I had beautiful hands too, just like Grandma.

As I rolled the pencil between my fingers, thoughts rolled around in my head.

Does wearing the right clothes or having a pretty face make you beautiful?

I suppose that might be true, if how people looked on the outside was the only thing that counts.

That's how Little Red Riding Hood saw things when she met the wolf all dressed up in Grandma's clothes. She didn't look beyond the pajamas to see the villain underneath.

There's a problem with just looking on the outside, I believe. You can take the outside stuff on and off, like makeup. Or Pickle clothes. But that stuff is fake, like that four-leaf clover I thought I found.

I want the kind of beauty you can't buy in

a store—and doesn't come off with soap—because it's right there in your heart.

Taking a big breath, I began drawing. I drew my hair gray, extra long, and braided. Perfect hair for grandchildren to use as a jump rope.

I drew lots of tiny wrinkles on my face. Wrinkles I will not trade for anything because they will remind me of the smiles God's brought into my life and the worries God's carried me through.

I drew bumpy hands, all rough from washing off boo-boos, cleaning up messes, praying, and knitting fuzzy, blue mittens.

I drew sparkles in my eyes. As long as I look inside myself and remember to laugh, I don't think I will ever lose those sparkles.

I stopped for a moment to shake crayon-holding cramps out of my hands.

Almost done.

With my best spelling, I wrote, "When I am seventy-five years old, I will have gray hair and wrinkles. I will have big hands. I will be full of surprises. And I will be so beautiful."

I paused, and then added, "Just like I am beautiful now."

Even though I knew Lynette and Kayla were waiting for me to call, I decided to count my sentences first, just to make sure I wrote enough to make Mrs. Arnold happy.

Plus, I wanted to read them again.

One more time.

Mom stepped into the room, carrying a load of laundry. She dumped the basket on the table and started sorting clothes. "Aren't you done with that assignment yet?"

I held up a finger before answering. I

didn't want to lose count. "Five. Wowie. Five sentences! What will Mrs. Arnold think?"

Turning a sock inside-out, Mom said, "She'll think you worked really hard on it."

I said, "I did work really hard on it." *All week long, in fact,* I thought.

It was time to call my friends.

But wait! First, I needed to get all dressed up.

So I did.

I put on my best smile.

Chatter Matters

1. What special events do you get all dressed up for? Why?

2. What do you think Meghan Rose meant when she said God sees and loves the YOU you? Describe a time when you felt loved by God.

3. What are five things you like about yourself? your brother or sister? a close friend? your mom or dad? your teacher? What things did you name the most often? What does that tell you about real beauty?

4. What does the Bible say about beauty? Look up 1 Corinthians 15:41 and Psalm 139. Explain to a parent what you think the verses mean. Then ask your parent to explain what he or she thinks they mean.

5. Colossians 3:12 says we should clothe ourselves with compassion, kindness, humility, gentleness, and patience. Explain what you think each piece of clothing on the list means, and how you can show that clothing with your actions.

Blam! – Great Activity Ideas

1. Make a crown. You need a pencil, a ruler, scissors, thin cardboard or construction paper, decorating supplies, and a stapler or tape.

Place the ruler across the cardboard or paper, near the bottom edge and lined up straight with that edge. Trace a straight line along the upper edge of the ruler lengthwise across the cardboard. Draw some triangles or other shapes across the top line to make it look like a crown.

Cut out your crown drawing. Decorate the crown shape with paper, lace, sequins, buttons, stickers, markers, or whatever decoration supplies you have on hand.

Finally, curl the crown around your head and ask an adult to staple or tape the ends of the crown together so it fits around your head.

2. Make a pasta necklace using a long piece of yarn and colored pasta. To color the pasta, you need newspaper, a small plastic bag, food coloring, rubbing alcohol, and pasta (wheels, elbow, or penne).

In a small plastic bag, mix 1 teaspoon of food coloring with $1/8$ cup rubbing alcohol. (Add more food coloring for darker color.) Add $1/2$ cup of pasta to the bag and close it tight. Carefully shake the bag until pasta is evenly coated. Spread pasta onto the newspaper and allow it to dry.

Once dry, tie one piece of pasta on the end of the yarn (leaving a three-inch tail) to prevent the other pieces from sliding off.

Then string on the pasta! When you have a string as long as you want, tie the ends of the yarn together to complete the necklace.

3. Make a mirror. You need cardboard (a cereal box works nicely), two different-sized round items to trace (like a plate and a cup), a pencil, a ruler, glue, construction paper, decorating supplies, and aluminum foil.

Trace the larger round object near the top of the cardboard. Lay the ruler down so one end of it touches the bottom of the circle you traced. Trace both edges of the ruler to make a handle for your mirror. Cut out the cardboard mirror shape.

Place the larger round item on aluminum foil, trace around it, and cut out that foil circle. Glue this foil circle shiny side out onto the large round part of the cardboard mirror.

Then use the cardboard mirror to trace another mirror shape onto construction paper. Cut out the construction paper mirror.

Center the smaller round item in the middle of the round part of the construction paper mirror and trace around the item. Cut out this smaller circle to leave a hole in the middle of the construction paper mirror.

Glue the back side of the construction paper onto the cardboard mirror shape. The foil should show through the center. Decorate your mirror with beads, buttons, stickers . . . even colored pasta!

4. Make snickerdoodle cookies with a parent or other grown-up. In a large bowl, mix the following ingredients together very well: 1 cup soft butter, 1½ cups sugar, and 2 eggs.

In a separate bowl, sift together 2¾ cups flour, 2 teaspoons cream of tartar, ¼ teaspoon salt, and 1 teaspoon baking soda. Blend the flour mixture into the butter mixture well.

Roll the dough into 1-inch balls. Mix 2 tablespoons sugar with 2 teaspoons cinnamon. Roll each ball into the cinnamon and sugar mixture.

Place the balls 2 inches apart on an ungreased baking sheet. Bake each batch at 400 degrees for 8–10 minutes until lightly browned but still soft.

Lori Scott, a graduate of Wheaton College and former first grade teacher, loves creative science and math activities, drama and art, the Sunday comics, and . . . red pens!

Lori has published numerous devotions, short stories, poems, articles, and puzzles for children, teens, and adults. Although she created the Meghan Rose series for her daughter, Meghan, her son, Michael, enjoys reading the books too.

Look for more Meghan Rose secrets and surprises online at www.MeghanRoseSeries.com!

Stacy Curtis is a cartoonist, illustrator, and printmaker whose illustrations have appeared in several magazines, newspapers, and children's books.

Stacy grew up in Kentucky and graduated with a degree in graphic design from Western Kentucky University. He and his wife, Jann, now live in Oak Lawn, Illinois and happily share their home with their dog, Derby. Stacy's artwork can be found on the Web at www.stacycurtis.com.